Cricket Rules OK
The Laws of Cricket

Cricket Rules OK
The Laws of Cricket

Geoff Hales

Illustrations by Bryan Flaherty

A & C Black · London

To Arthur Morgan, John Hill and the Remnants

First published 1986 by
A & C Black (Publishers) Limited
35 Bedford Row, London WC1R 4JH

Hales, Geoff
    Cricket rules OK : the laws of cricket
    1. Cricket — Rules
    I. Title
    796.35'8'02022   GV925

    ISBN 0-7136-5538-0

Printed and bound in Great Britain by
A. Wheaton Co. & Ltd, Exeter.

Acknowledgement
Printed by permission of MCC. Copies of the modern edition of
the Laws of Cricket with full notes and interpretations can be
obtained from MCC at Lord's Cricket Ground, London NW8.
Price 50p excluding postage.

Contents

Introduction

Cricket is the greatest game in the world — no one should dispute that. Cricket is a simple game, too. A bowler bowls a ball at a batsman, who tries to hit it. If he succeeds, he can set out to run to the other end of a pitch twenty-two yards long. If he gets there before the ball comes back, he scores one run. Most of us know that the ball weighs between 5½ ounces (155.9 grams) and 5¾ ounces (163 grams), and measures between 8¹³⁄₁₆ inches (22.4 cm) and 9 inches (22.9 cm) in circumference. The bat, as anyone will tell you, must not be more than 38 inches (96.5 cm) long, and the blade must be made of wood and must not exceed 4¼ inches (10.8 cm) at its widest point. In trying to hit the ball, the batsman must make sure that he is not out — bowled, timed out, caught, handled the ball, hit the ball twice, hit wicket, leg before wicket, obstructing the field, run out or stumped. To complete a run the batsman must have 'some part of his bat in his hand or of his person . . . grounded behind the line of the popping crease' before a fielder breaks the wicket with the ball, the hand holding the ball, or the arm of the hand holding the ball. No problems there.

Unfortunately, a lot of players, and players who are obliged to stand for a few overs as makeshift umpires, are unfamiliar with the Laws, even with the most important ones. No one is likely to have to weigh a ball or measure a bat, but everyone ought to know that the batsman must be *behind* the line of the popping crease to be 'in', and what the Law on LBW really is. Much bad feeling is caused when temporary umpires apply what they think is the Law to batsmen and bowlers who are sure they know better, when in fact neither party knows what it is talking about. Bats get thrown in dressing-rooms, sulks curdle the milk at tea, and people are left out of rounds. Games can be spoilt like this.

Clubs could do more about the problem by encouraging players to develop the attitude that a sound knowledge of the Laws is just as important as playing skills. They could invite qualified umpires to talk at meetings in the winter. They could organise quizzes on points of law, perhaps against other clubs, and make sure that a copy of the Laws is available in the pavilion for players to browse through in their rare moments of idleness. And clubs could be more firm with players who do not accept umpires' decisions at once.

This book is not intended as a substitute for a thorough study of *The Laws of Cricket*, published by MCC. It is intended to wipe out a few myths or misunderstandings of the sort that cause problems on the field, in the dressing-room, and in the bar afterwards. All the Laws I refer to are printed at the end of the book by my generous and discerning publisher, and courtesy of MCC.

The Umpires

The word 'umpire' originally meant something like 'one who is without equals'. This is comforting.

Umpires are fine, upright characters who are prepared to stand for hours in the middle of a field giving difficult decisions which require the finest judgment. They are then treated with suspicion by players who know that their old grannies could do a better job. The umpire's only solace is that he is sure to be asked again next week because nobody else ever wants to do it.

This is not a book on umpiring, but almost everyone who plays is bound from time to time to have to put on a white coat and dole out happiness or misery to his fellow creatures. The first qualification for the task is a comprehensive knowledge of the Laws: the umpire will command respect only if it is clear that he knows what he is doing.

The umpires should always be neutral and willing to stand. Ideally they should stand for the whole match, and be bought a drink at close of play as a mark of appreciation. They should not be recruited in the pub a few minutes before (or after) the start; and they should not be conscripts from the lower order of the batting side. Of course there are many matches where this is unavoidable. When players act as umpires, they ought not to be regarded as 'our umpire' and 'their umpire' — they are just officials. 'Well, their umpire gave it, so they can't complain' is often heard: the umpires are not a part of the team, and cries of 'Good old James!' when an appeal is upheld or turned down are not helpful, least of all to the umpire.

Whatever your personal habits, when umpiring you should be smartly dressed and properly equipped. Leave your beer and your cigarettes in the care of a friend (greater love hath no man than this . . .) Check that you have six (or eight) counters, and a spare in an inside pocket (so that it doesn't get mixed up with the others). Don't drop them. Grubbing round in the grass for a lost coin, matchstick, stone, piece of Lego, etc. does nothing for your reputation as a competent and fearless dispenser of justice. It's also useful to have something to wipe a

wet ball with. You should have a spare ball, spare bails,
a bowler's marker, pencil and paper, a watch that works
and a thick skin.

The umpire should give decisions clearly and firmly,
and should not be drawn into explanations, justifications
and arguments at the time or later. It is not unknown
for players to assure the umpire that they could 'see it
from here', and to offer other, fanciful, interpretations of
the Laws for his benefit. But the umpire is the man who
makes the decisions; he has the best view and no axe to
grind. He must have enough self-confidence to disregard
the hysterical bowler, the batsman who rubs his thigh
meaningfully, and the deep extra cover who is sure he
heard the faint inside edge. He must make the decision
on the basis of what he himself saw. All appeals,
however frivolous, must be taken seriously and answered
politely. 'Not out' is the usual phrase, though I have
heard 'Come off it, mate!' and 'Give it a rest!' from hard-
pressed umpires with a gift for repartee. The umpire
must also have the courage to call 'no ball' in whatever
circumstances it occurs.

If the umpire is a member of the batting side, he must
try to forget his team loyalties and his private emotions.
He shouldn't whistle at near misses and laugh out loud
at dropped catches. His own wish to bat or not to bat

should not influence his decisions. He must show his impartiality by resisting the temptation to coach and applaud the batsmen. Our all-rounder, Fred the Finger, who umpires a lot of our games, earned himself a good deal of unpopularity in this way in the annual match against *The Duck and Firkin*. He refused to give a run-out decision against his brother, George, who represented our best chance of winning a run-chase. He was perfectly entitled to do this of course, and he made the decision as clearly and firmly as you could wish; but what soured the atmosphere was that it was Fred who had called the batsmen for two from square leg and it was Fred who led the rather restrained applause when George reached his fifty.

Every player and potential umpire should read *The Laws of Cricket* as published by MCC. *Cricket Umpiring and Scoring* by Tom Smith (Dent, 1980) is also invaluable, and comprehensive.

This book concentrates on some of the Laws which are most often misunderstood and misquoted. Now read on. Knowledge is power . . .

Ground conditions (Law 3.8)

The umpires must decide whether conditions are fit for play, but if both the captains want to play, in spite of the conditions, they have the right to insist on playing. The umpires must regard conditions as unfit only if they are actually dangerous to the players. The umpires should check to see that the bowlers' footmarks are reasonably secure, that the fielders can move safely, at least in the in-field (within about thirty yards of the pitch), and that the batsmen can play the ball normally and can run between the wickets. They should also see that there are no pools of water on the pitch or the in-field. If they are satisfied, play should take place. Naturally, the advice of the groundsman should be taken, and if he says that play is impossible, this must be accepted.

Weather (Law 3.8)

In the unlikely event of rain falling in a cricket season,
the umpires may decide that it is too heavy for play to
continue. Very heavy rain usually causes an infantry
charge to the nearest shelter anyway, but the correct
procedure is for the umpires to consult the fielding
captain and the batsmen. It may be that one side will
want to continue and press for a victory, while the other
will be only too glad to come off and escape with a draw.
If the fielding captain and the batsmen disagree, play is
suspended. It can continue only if both sides really want
to slug it out in the rain.

Bad light (Law 3.8)

Bad light is nearly as unlikely as rain, but if the umpires think that the light is too poor for play to continue safely, they will offer the batsmen the chance to leave the field till it improves. The fielding side is not asked what it thinks; the danger is considered to be to the batsmen. If the batsmen choose to stay on, they or their captain may appeal against the light at any later stage, and if the umpires think the light has become worse since the batsmen agreed to continue, they will take the players off. The fielding side has no right to appeal against the light at any time.

It is entirely up to the umpires to judge when and whether play starts again after a stoppage, and the players are expected to resume without delay once the umpires are satisfied with the conditions. During a stoppage the umpires should check regularly to see if there has been an improvement, and should get the game started again as soon as possible.

Boundaries (Law 19)

It is important that the umpires and captains agree before start of play what the boundaries are and how they are marked. On most grounds this is obvious; but in parks, for instance, where there may be no line, rope, board or fence, it will have to be agreed whether the boundary is a path, a line of benches or trees, the end of the grass or an imaginary line between posts, flags or other clearly defined points.

The umpires must also agree as to whether obstacles within the playing area are to be regarded as boundaries. 'Persons' may be treated as boundaries as well, and if this is agreed, a boundary is scored if the ball hits a wandering tourist or a horizontal courting couple, or if a spectator picks up the ball before it crosses the line. A sight-screen within the playing area is a boundary too, but to score six, the ball must clear it. A full-pitch hit into the screen scores only four.

Local tradition, which must always be respected, may allow for a tree to be within or overhanging the playing

area without being a boundary. The ball does not become dead when it hits such a tree. Runs may continue to be scored and catches can be taken from rebounds. Another local custom may be that only four is scored when the ball is hit without bouncing over a very short boundary.

Dead ball (Law 23)

There are several situations when a ball automatically becomes 'dead' and it is not necessary to call and signal 'dead ball'. These include when the ball is 'finally settled in the hands of the Wicket-Keeper or the Bowler', when it goes for four or six, when it lodges in a batman's pads or clothing or in the clothing of an umpire, or in a fielder's helmet. It also becomes 'dead' automatically when a batsman is out, when 'lost ball' is called, when the ball is fielded illegally, and at the call of 'over' or 'time'. It becomes 'live' again when the bowler begins his run-up to bowl the next ball.

There are a number of situations in which the umpires should call 'dead ball'. These include cases of unfair play, and serious injury. The ball must also be called 'dead' if the batsman is not ready to take strike and does not try to play the ball, or if the bails fall from the striker's wicket before the ball arrives, or if the bowler drops the ball before delivery or does not let it go for some reason (such as getting his run-up wrong). In addition, the umpire calls 'dead ball' if he goes to consult his colleague, or when he disallows leg-byes. Leg-byes, incidentally, are allowed only if the batsman has tried to play the ball with the bat, or has been hit trying to avoid it. If the batsmen attempt a run from a leg-bye which is going to be disallowed, the umpire delays the call until one 'run' has been completed. This gives the fielders the chance to run the batsmen out. When the 'run' is completed, the batsmen go back to their original ends and the run does not count (Law 26).

The ball is not dead if it rebounds from an umpire, or hits the stumps without the batsman being out. It

B. FLAHERTY

remains live if an appeal is turned down or if the batsman accidentally knocks the stumps down in running, or the bowler does so in delivering the ball. The ball does not become dead on the call of 'no ball' or 'wide'.

The only difficulty here is to judge when the ball is 'finally settled'. Just being held by the wicket-keeper or the bowler is not enough. The batsmen may still be running or out of their ground, and there may be the chance of a wicket. The ball should be called 'dead' only if it is clear that there is no possibility of further runs or of a wicket falling.

Appeals (Law 27)

Many decisions are so clear-cut that it is hardly necessary for the umpire to lift his finger, but it has to be remembered that a batsman cannot be given out unless there is an appeal. The batsman has every right

to stand his ground until an appeal is made and he is given out. It is a graceful act, however, to 'walk' if you know you have edged the ball and the umpire is in doubt.

The Law actually specifies 'How's that?' as the universal form of appeal. You do not need to tell the umpire what you are appealing for. In fact, if you ask 'How's that for stumped?' the umpire will have to turn the appeal down if a run-out has taken place. A polite enquiry is just as likely to get results as screaming in the umpire's ear when he is weighing up what happened and trying to make a good decision.

An appeal can be made at any time before the bowler begins his run-up for the next ball, even if 'over' has been called and the ball is the first of the next over. It is too late to appeal, however, when the umpire has called 'time' and removed the bails before an interval or an interruption of play, or at the end of the day's play or at

the end of the match. You cannot give a man out at the tea table.

The bowler's end umpire is responsible for answering all appeals except those for hit wicket, stumped and run out at the striker's end, which are clearly the duty of the square leg umpire. An appeal which is made to the 'wrong' umpire can simply be answered 'not out' but the umpire could, in the interests of a fair decision, refer the appealer to the other umpire, who will then answer the appeal. The rejection of an appeal for, say, LBW, does not mean that a second appeal cannot be made for a stumping or a catch, since the batsman may be given out for that.

The umpires should consult on points of fact if one is in a better position than the other to see what happened. If there is still any doubt after a brief conference, the batsman is not out.

The umpire can change his decision if he does so without delay, and he can allow the fielding captain to withdraw an appeal after the batsman has been given out, as long as the batsman has not left the field. The umpire must also recall a batsman who has begun that long, sad, solitary walk back, under the impression that he has been given out when in fact he has not.

Batting with a runner (Laws 2.5, 2.6 and 2.7)

A batsman can have the services of a runner if he is injured or ill in the course of the match. The runner must be a member of the batting side, if possible one who has batted already (so that a batsman still to come in does not get a sneak preview of the conditions and a look at the bowling) and he must wear gloves and pads, as long as the injured batsman is also wearing them (if he's not, then the runner doesn't have to use them either). He does not have to wear a helmet, even if the batsman is wearing one.

Batting with a runner causes problems about where everyone should stand. When the injured batsman is taking strike, the runner should go to square leg. The square leg umpire should stay on the off side; he must always be in a position to see the action. When the

injured batsman has played and a run is in progress, he should retreat to square leg and stay there till he needs to take strike again. He is considered to be out of the game except when taking strike, and if he brings himself into it, he risks being given out for 'any transgression'. The runner, on reaching the non-striker's end, takes up the usual non-striker's position.

The injured batsman is out if his runner handles the ball, wilfully obstructs the field or is run out. He may of course be out in all the usual ways, with the additional peril that he may be run out or stumped if he leaves his ground or starts involuntarily on a run, forgetting that he has a runner, and regardless of whether the runner is 'in' at the time. He may also be run out if the runner is out of his ground when he himself is playing the ball, even if he, the injured batsman, never left the crease. In other words, both batsman and runner must be careful not to wander; either one can be run out.

The Bowlers

Bowlers are emotional, impulsive creatures, quick to applaud a generous decision but liable to take offence when the umpires venture to disagree with them. Any number of painful misunderstandings could be avoided if the bowlers knew what the Laws really say and relied less on folk-lore.

No ball (Law 24)

There are a lot of myths about this. The truth is relatively simple. To avoid bowling a no ball:

☐ The bowler must tell the umpire when he plans to change his 'mode of delivery'; for example, when he switches from bowling over the wicket to bowling round, or from bowling right arm to bowling left.

☐ The ball must not be thrown, and the straightening of the arm must occur well before the ball is released. Either umpire must call 'no ball' if he 'is not entirely satisfied with the absolute fairness of a delivery in this respect'.

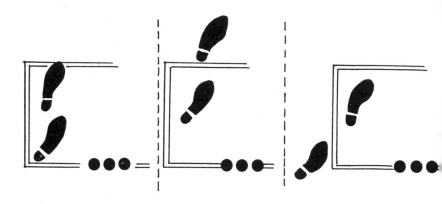

☐ In the delivery stride, the bowler's back foot must land inside the return crease or its forward extension without touching it, and some part of the front foot (even if it is not on the ground) must be behind the popping crease.

'No ball' must also be called if, at the moment of delivery, the wicket-keeper or fielders are infringing Laws about where they may stand; that is, the wicket-keeper must remain entirely behind the wicket, there must not be more than two fielders behind square (i.e. the line of the popping crease) on the leg side, and no fielder should be standing on the pitch, or 'have any part of his person extended over the pitch' (as Law 41 puts it). Also, it should be remembered that a batsman can be run out, or given out hit the ball twice, handled the ball and obstructing the field from a 'no ball'. Bouncers and beamers may be penalised by the call of 'no ball' as well (Law 42).

Wide (Law 25)

A ball is wide if it passes so high over or wide of the wicket that in the umpire's opinion the batsman, in his normal guard position, cannot reach it. The umpire must take into account the height and reach of the batsman when making a decision. A wide to a very small batsman

may not be one to a very tall batsman. The batsman must not try to make a ball into a wide by moving to a position from which he cannot reach it; if he moves towards it he brings it within his reach and the ball is not then wide.

Other things to remember about wides include:

☐ A ball must not be called a wide until it has passed the line of the striker's wicket. If it stops before reaching him, the batsman has the right to make one attempt to hit the stationary ball, without interference from the fielders. 'Wide' is not called.

☐ The striker can be out hit wicket or stumped from a wide. Either batsman can be run out or given out handled the ball or obstructing the field. Even if a batsman is out off a wide, the penalty of one run still stands.

Fred the Finger had a galling experience a few years ago over the matter of a wide that wasn't. He was bowling and was well on his way to his five wickets for the season when his flipper got out of control and set off for point. The umpire called 'wide', the batsman strode gleefully forwards, hit the ball second bounce, and was caught. Fred appealed and was told that you cannot be caught off a wide, which was true as far as it went. Fred, who happened to know the Law, pointed out that the ball had not passed the line of the striker's wicket and so could not be called a wide, and in any case the batsman had brought the ball within his reach by chasing it. The batsman chipped in at this point and said that once 'wide' had been called, he could do what he liked, and, in his considered opinion, it wasn't out. The umpire agreed and the batsman stayed. In fact, the umpire should never have called 'wide' at all, and having done so, should have revoked the call as soon as the ball came within the batsman's reach. The ball would then have become a normal, legal delivery and Fred would have got his wicket. As it was, he was still two short at the end of the season.

B. FLAHERTY

Bouncers and beamers (Law 42)

It is unfair to bowl fast, short-pitched balls (bouncers) in an attempt to intimidate the batsman. 'As a guide', the Law says, 'a fast short-pitched ball is one which pitches short and passes, or would have passed, above the shoulder height of the Striker standing in a normal batting stance at the crease'. 'Intimidating' means the intention or likelihood of injuring the batsman. The umpire takes the batsman's skill into account. This is to save the unrecognised batsman from becoming unrecognisable. In the case of a beamer (a fast, high, full-pitch) the umpire must be satisfied that it was

deliberate, aimed at the batsman, and above shoulder height.

The umpire may act at once in the event of intimidatory bowling. He is not obliged to give the bowler any preliminary warning, though he may do. If he considers that a delivery is unfair, he will call 'no ball' and then warn the bowler formally. He must tell the other umpire, the batsmen and the fielding captain. If the bowler persists he is 'no-balled' again, and given a

final warning. If he really cannot take a hint and bowls yet another unfair ball, he is again 'no-balled' and is at once taken off without completing the over, which must be completed by someone else. The bowler is not allowed to bowl again in that innings, even from the other end. At a suitable interval the umpire will report the matter to the captain of the batting side and to the club and league authorities, who are told by the Law to take 'any further action which is considered to be appropriate . . .'

Running down the pitch (Law 42)

Running down the pitch after delivering the ball is likely to damage it in a way that will help other bowlers. It is therefore considered to be unfair play. The area that the umpires must protect from trampling feet is considered to begin four feet from the popping crease (front line) and to extend one foot either side of the line of the middle stump. However, umpires must do what they can to prevent damage to any area of the pitch, even outside the specified area, if they think the resulting mess may be of assistance to another bowler.

If the umpire thinks the bowler is damaging the pitch in this way, he must caution him, give him a final warning, have him taken off and report him — the same procedure as for dealing with bouncers and beamers, except that the bowler is not no-balled for trespassing. Some comfort for bowlers here is that fielders and even batsmen who damage the pitch can be chastised too, though not sent off or given out.

Lifting the seam (Law 42)

Bowlers are not allowed to alter the condition of the ball by lifting the seam. This constitutes unfair play as well. The umpires are required to inspect the ball frequently and at irregular intervals, and if they find that the seam is being 'picked' they must change the ball for one with an unraised seam but which is otherwise in the same condition as the vandalised one. Bowlers are also not allowed to polish the ball with 'any artificial substance' (sweat is permitted).

Trial run-ups (Law 15)

A final prohibition in this section on things bowlers must not do if they want people to like them is that the Law on start of play prevents bowlers from having a trial run-up after the call of 'play', except at the fall of a wicket, when the umpire may allow it if he thinks that no time will be wasted and no damage caused to the pitch.

Apart from the above, most things that are not actually forbidden are usually permitted.

The Batsmen

Batsmen are sensitive and suspicious souls who tend to question the legal bases of their dismissals on returning earlier than expected to the judicial calm of the dressing-room. Knowing the Laws is no comfort in these trying circumstances, but that is no reason for not knowing them. So in this section and the next the Laws about 'out' are looked at.

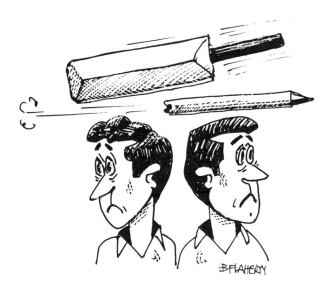

Leg before wicket (Law 36)

LBW causes more PMT (Post Match Trouble) than anything else, and there are more theories about it than there are stories about Fred Trueman. The Law clearly states what must happen before the batsman can be given out leg before wicket:
☐ The ball must have pitched in a straight line between wicket and wicket, or outside the line of the off-stump. In the case of a full pitch, the umpire must be satisfied that it would have pitched in line.

☐ The ball must strike the batsman at a point in a straight line between wicket and wicket even if it is too high at the moment of impact. If the ball is too high, the umpire must be satisfied that it was going down and was going on to hit the stumps.

☐ The umpire must be satisfied that the ball would have hit the stumps.

There is one exception. If the batsman was playing no stroke, he can be given out LBW even if he is struck outside the line of the off-stump. Again, of course, the umpire must be sure that the ball was going on to hit the wicket.

You cannot be given out LBW if you first intercept the ball with your bat or the hand holding the bat. And you cannot be out LBW to a ball pitching outside the line of the leg stump, whatever it does afterwards.

The myths about LBW, repeated with the utmost sincerity and conviction by wise old heads after their third pint, include:

☐ 'Couldn't have been out — he was bowling round.' But the Law says nothing about this. What matters is where the ball pitched, where it struck the batsman and whether it would have hit the stumps. Where it was bowled from is irrelevant.

☐ 'Couldn't have been out — he was bowling leggies.' But the eccentricities of the bowler have nothing to do with it.

☐ 'Couldn't have been out — I was right forward.' But being on the front foot does not save you from the awful majesty of Law 36. It may sow doubts in the umpire's mind about the final destination of the ball, but that is all. If in any doubt, he must of course give the batsman not out.

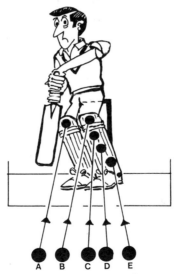

A Not out (unless no stroke was being played and the ball would have hit the stumps)

B Out (the ball struck the batsman in line and would have hit the stumps)

C Out (the ball pitched in line, hit in line and would have hit the stumps)

D Out (for exactly the same reasons as C)

E Not out (the ball pitched outside the line of the leg stump)

☐ 'I was playing a stroke.' But that will save you only if the ball hit you outside the line of off-stump.

☐ 'It pitched outside off.' But even if it did, you can still be out if the ball hit you in line and would have hit the stumps.

☐ 'It hit me outside off.' But if you weren't playing a stroke and the ball would have hit the stumps, that's out.

☐ 'It hit me way above the pad.' But if you were in line, and the ball was going down at the time and would have hit the stumps, that's out — even if it hit you on the head.

Fred got himself disliked again when we played *The Old Frog*. He gave an LBW decision against the world's slowest batsman, Prodder Pryke, who was only 48 short of his maiden 50. For months afterwards, Prodder explained to anyone who would listen that he could not have been LBW because he was so far down the wicket when the ball hit him that he could have patted Fred's guide-dog. Fred justified himself at regular intervals over the next season or two by saying that though the ball might have pitched just outside leg, it had turned very sharply and straightened. They were both wrong.

Bowled (Law 30)

It hardly seems necessary to say anything about that dreadful sound which the batsman hears in nightmares as well as in real life, the smash of leather on wood. You are out if the wicket is bowled down. There are one or two complications, however. If you play the ball and then kick or hit it on to the stumps and break them in an attempt to get back and avoid being stumped or run out, you are not out. What matters here is whether or not you have completed the stroke. But if you kick or hit the ball on to the stumps and break them in an attempt to protect them, you are out, whether or not you have completed the stroke. This is a difficult one for the umpire, who has to judge your intention.

The wicket is down (Law 28) only if a bail is completely removed from the top of the stumps. That is, if the bail is moved from its groove but goes back into it, or somehow remains on the top of the stumps, the wicket is not down and the batsman is not out. But in the event of the bail being removed from the top of the stumps and lodging between them without falling to the ground, the batsman is out: the bail is no longer on the top of the stumps. Not that this happens often. But history tells us of a Mr E. Winter who, in 1832, mis-cut and drove the bails deep into the stumps. He was not out.

Timed out (Law 31)

A new batsman may be given out, on appeal, if he deliberately takes more than two minutes to come in. This is to prevent a batting side in a tight situation from wasting time. The two minutes start from the fall of the previous wicket, and 'coming in' means stepping onto the field of play (i.e. crossing the boundary line), not taking guard or being ready to take strike. The umpire must

investigate the cause of the batsman's late arrival and must be satisfied that the delay is wilful; the side suffering a collapse and owning only three pairs of pads, one pair of left-handed batting gloves and no spare boxes cannot be penalised for lack of kit.

Handled the ball (Law 33)

This is a very unusual way of losing your wicket, but a batsman can be out if at any time while the ball is in play he touches it 'with the hand not holding the bat' and without the fielders' permission. If, for instance, he plays the ball down in front of him, picks it up without permission and throws it back, he can be given out on appeal. It is unlikely that anyone would appeal in these circumstances, but it could happen and the umpire would have to give it out. If you are struck on the hand, or if you involuntarily protect your face with your hand from a rising ball, that is not out. The handling must be wilful. If the ball lodges in the batsman's pads, it is dead

and the batsman is then free to remove it.

You can be out 'handled the ball' from a no ball (and for hitting the ball twice, and for obstruction).

Hit the ball twice (Law 34)

This is another situation when you can be given out for trying to help. You can be out for hitting the ball back to the bowler or to a fielder if you have already played it or stopped it in some other way, and have not asked the fielders' permission. You are allowed to hit the ball twice but only in the defence of the wicket, and even then you must not obstruct a fielder from making a catch. In 1624, Jasper Vinall of Horsham was killed preventing a batsman from having a second hit, so be warned.

Hit wicket (Law 35)

The batsman is out if he breaks the wicket with the bat or with 'any part of his person, dress, or equipment' at any time after the bowler begins his run-up (when the ball becomes 'live') until he sets off for his first run 'immediately after playing, or playing at, the ball'. He is also out if he breaks his wicket while making a second stroke to defend it. He cannot be out hit wicket while he is running (except at the start of the first run) or in avoiding being run out or stumped, or in avoiding a throw-in. In other words, once he has finished playing the ball and has set out for the first run, if there is one, he is safe from Law 35. He can, however, be out if he is injured and falls onto the wicket, although in the case of what appears to be a serious injury, he may be saved by the umpire calling 'dead ball' before the wicket is broken. If the call comes first, the batsman is not out. This may or may not be a comfort to him.

Obstructing the field (Law 37)

Being given out for this is a very rare occurrence. Accidental obstruction sometimes occurs, but the Law

makes it clear that a batsman must 'wilfully' obstruct the opposition 'by word or action' to be given out. 'Wilful' obstruction can include deliberately running into fielders or distracting a fielder who is trying to take a catch. A shout of 'Drop it!' is definitely wilful obstruction. If the non-striker obstructs the fielder from making a catch, it is the striker who is out. In other circumstances it is the offending batsman who has to go. Of course, there are cases where the obstruction is clearly not deliberate, for example when the non-striker gets in the way of a hard, very straight drive, or a throw-in hits either batsman. This is not out; moreover the ball does not become dead, and runs may be scored. The only case where the batsman can be given out when he is not intending to obstruct is if, in making a second stroke to defend his wicket, he prevents a catch from being made.

The terrors of run out, caught and stumped lurk in the next section.

The Fielders

Fielders are fair-minded and sociable chaps who congregate at the fall of a wicket, or at the end of an over in which they think one ought to have fallen, to congratulate the umpire on his impartiality and keen eyesight, or to assure the bowler that the umpire is corrupt and visually handicapped — they see no inconsistency in this.

Run out (Law 38)

You are out, of course, if you fail to 'make your ground' and 'the wicket is broken'. Both these phrases need some clarification. The batsman is out of his ground (Law 29) if no part of the bat (held in the hand) or of his person is grounded behind the line of the popping crease. It is not enough to be on the line, you must be behind it. The wicket can be broken (Law 28) by the ball directly, the hand holding the ball or even the arm of the hand holding the ball. The fielder cannot break the wicket with one hand or arm while holding the ball in the other hand. If a bail is already off, as it may be when a throw has hit the stumps and gone for overthrows, the wicket can be put down by removing the other bail or pulling or striking out of the ground any of the stumps. If both bails are off, a stump must be pulled or struck out of the ground. It is not enough just to hit them again. If all the stumps are already down, the fielders may put one or more back to give themselves the chance to break the wicket.

There is often some confusion about who is out when there is a really serious breakdown in negotiations, leaving one or both batsman stranded in the middle, or, worse, at one end. The Law explains that if the batsmen have crossed then the batsman who is running to the wicket that is broken is out. If they have not crossed, then the batsman leaving the broken wicket is the one destined for the early pint. If a batsman does not leave

his ground, or leaves it to start a run, changes his mind, goes back and is joined there by his partner, it is his partner who is out.

The batsman cannot be out if, having made his ground, he then steps out of it or lifts his bat out of it to avoid injury from a throw-in or a collision with a fielder. He is allowed to save his life without losing his wicket. He can be out if he backs up too far and the bowler runs him out at the end of his run-up. The bowler is perfectly entitled to do this and is not obliged to give the batsman any warning, though bowlers usually do. Running out in this way is supposed to be 'not cricket', but it is also against the spirit of the game to steal runs by backing up too far.

If the bowler throws the ball in an attempt to run out the non-striker in this way and misses, the batsmen may then run, and any runs are scored as no balls. If the bowler does not try to run out the non-striker and the batsmen attempt a run, the umpire calls 'dead ball' as soon as the batsmen have crossed, and no run is allowed.

You can also be run out from a no ball.

Caught (Law 32)

'Caught' is in itself a simple enough idea. The ball sticks, the batsman goes and you know that this is the best game in the world and it's a privilege to be playing it with such splendid team-mates. Put it down and only the thought of cutting the grass at the weekend stops you from giving up cricket altogether. It's delirium or Dostoevsky.

But the definition of 'a fair catch' needs a little study. For a fair catch to have been made, the Law insists that the fielder must have 'complete control over the further disposal of the ball' and that he must remain 'within the field of play'.

There is no precise measure of when the ball comes under complete control, and there is no definite time limit for which the ball has to be retained, but it is clear that the fielder who hurls the ball upwards in triumph in the act of catching it risks a 'not out' decision on the grounds that the catch is not completed. This need not

be a problem — most of the players I know are so relieved not to have dropped the ball that they part with it very reluctantly. Remember the ones you put down, and hold on to it.

Being within the field of play means that the fielder must not be on, behind or even touching a boundary line or a rope on the ground, though he may lean over it to make the catch. When the boundary is marked by a board or fence, or a rope raised from the ground, however, the fielder may touch it and even lean on it or over it to make a catch, as long as he does not ground any part of himself behind it. It is very difficult for the umpire to see this. He is necessarily far from that particular piece of action and must also be watching for short runs and other activity on the pitch. He may have to rely on the honesty of the fielder. In this, and in any other matter where he is not sure of the facts, he should consult the other umpire. If not satisfied that the catch was fairly made, the umpires must give the batsman not out and signal six.

The batsman can be caught if the ball deflects off either hand or glove, below the wrist, provided that the hand struck is on the bat at the time. On or above the

wrist of hand or glove is not out. The batsman is out, too, if caught off any part of his person or equipment, including his helmet, as long as the ball also touches the bat or the hand or glove below the wrist.

The batsman is also fairly caught by a fielder who hugs the ball to his body in an agonised embrace like something out of D. H. Lawrence, or if it lodges accidentally 'in his dress' or in the wicket-keeper's pads. If it lodges in a helmet worn by a fielder (perhaps in the visor) that is not out and 'dead ball' is called. An unlikely event, but it's always as well to know these things.

Catches can be made after a deflection off the non-striker, an umpire or another fielder, as long as the ball has not touched a fielder's helmet. You can catch a ball off a fielder's head, but not off his helmet. If the ball lodges in the umpire's clothing, or in the clothing or equipment of either batsman, 'dead ball' must be called.

It is also possible to make a fair catch off any obstruction within the field of play, such as a tree or any overhanging branches of a tree whose trunk is outside the boundary, provided that it has not been agreed beforehand that the obstruction is a boundary. Local custom sometimes makes this possible. Usually, however, the umpires will have decided that anything really substantial inside the boundary line does constitute a boundary and the question will not arise.

As I said, 'caught' in itself is a simple enough idea . . .

Stumped (Law 39)

This is another easy one — the batsman is out if he misses the ball and is out of his ground when the wicket-keeper gathers the ball and breaks the wicket. In achieving this miracle of reflex and co-ordination, the keeper may break the wicket with the ball itself, the hand or glove holding the ball or even the arm of the

hand wearing the glove. He may kick or throw the ball on to the wicket, or it may be involuntarily deflected from his pads or any other part of his dress or equipment. He may not, however, take the ball in front of the stumps in an attempt to make a stumping unless the batsman has already played or stopped the ball. There is a distinction to make here between what is a stumping and what is a run-out. Unless the batsman is attempting a run, he is stumped, but if he is, he is run out. It is also not a stumping if any other fielder is involved in any way, even if the batsman is not attempting a run. This seems to be a good point, by the way, to remind batsmen that to be 'in their ground' they must have the bat or some part of themselves behind the popping crease — being only on the line will give the keeper his victim.

Fielding the ball (Law 41.1)

Fielders may use only their persons (any part of) in an attempt to field the ball, and wilful use of caps, sweaters, etc. will incur the call of 'dead ball'. Moreover, a penalty of five runs will be scored or added to the number of runs already scored off that ball, including the run in progress if the batsmen have already crossed. The same applies to a ball which hits a helmet put out to grass behind the stumps.

Limitation of on-side fielders (Law 41.2)

No more than two fielders are allowed to be behind square on the leg-side (that is, behind the line of the popping crease) at the moment the ball is delivered. If there are more than two, the square leg umpire must call 'no ball'. The two does not include the wicket-keeper, if for any reason he chooses to stand on the leg side.

Position of fieldsmen (Law 41.3)

The only other restriction on where fieldsmen stand is that no fielder may stand on the pitch or have 'any part of his person extended over' it until the ball has been played or has passed the bat. The pitch is defined as being 22 yards long and 10 feet wide, and is not exactly the same area that the bowler must not run on to. The umpire may also require that fielders whose shadows fall onto this area keep absolutely still, but if the batsman objects to their being there the captain will be expected to move the fielders. Law 40 (The Wicket-Keeper) makes it clear that the keeper must remain completely behind the wicket until the ball is played or stopped, or passes the line of the stumps. Again, the penalty for any infringement is a no ball, and the bowler can be expected to be none too pleased with any fielder who costs him a run in this way. The fielders have a duty here not only to play within the spirit of the game but to save their side from unnecessary penalty runs.

Obstruction of the batsman (Laws 42.6 and 42.7)

The batsman has the right to play the ball and defend his wicket without interference. Just as obstruction of the field by the batsman can be 'by word or action', so can the obstruction of the batsman by the fielders. Any noise or action by a fielder which 'incommodes the striker' while he is receiving the ball is unfair, and in this event the umpire will call 'dead ball'. This is intended to cover such things as fielders trying to 'talk the batsman out' by making unkind remarks about his personal appearance, the marital status of his parents and his chances of surviving the next delivery, or moving across his line of sight to distract him, at any time after the start of the bowler's run-up. The umpire must also call 'dead ball' if he considers that any fielder 'wilfully'

obstructs a batsman who is running. Any completed
runs are allowed, including the run in progress at the
time of the call, and any boundary.

Lost ball (Law 20)

It is very unlikely that a ball will be lost inside a
boundary, but there are cases recorded of balls being lost
or found in places from which they cannot be recovered.
I have heard of a ball being stuck in the nozzle of a
disused village pump which the umpires had neglected to
say was a boundary, and of a ball that got lodged in a
tree and did not come down till some years later when it
rotted. A ball that can be seen but not recovered is
regarded as 'lost'. The Law applies only to balls lost

inside the boundary; once the ball has left the playing area it automatically becomes dead.

Any fielder despairing of the situation may call 'lost ball', and this call is taken as final even if the ball is recovered immediately afterwards. The batsmen may of course run while the fielders are looking for the ball, and it soon becomes worth the fielders' while to declare the ball lost. On the call of 'lost ball', six runs are added to the score as it stood before the batsmen took the first run. So, if the batsmen have run five at the moment of the call, the score goes up by six, not eleven. If they have already run seven, however, seven runs are added (not thirteen). Any run in progress at the time of the call counts as long as the batsmen have crossed.

To summarise — if six or fewer than six have been run at the time of the call, the total goes up by six. If more that six have been run, then the total goes up by that number. The runs are credited to the batsman only if he has hit the ball — otherwise they count as extras.

Finally, polishing. Any fielder may polish the ball with any 'natural substance' (which excludes such things as hair oil). But the umpire will move in if he thinks you are doing it to waste time. So get a move on. And remember that you are not permitted to rub the ball on the ground, though you can dry it or remove mud from it.

The Captains

Captains are elected by their team-mates, who respect them for their amiability, seniority, tactical awareness and qualities of leadership. This respect lasts till well into the second week of the season. Then the captain will be revealed to his subjects for what they always thought he was, a morose upstart who couldn't organise a round of drinks. However, a captain who knows the Laws and leads his team in accordance with them will have at least his self-respect left at the end of the season.

In addition to the burdens that fall on anyone who aspires to be a leader of men, and even on the reluctant hero who has captaincy thrust upon him, it is up to the skipper to know the Laws better than anyone in the team. In particular he should know what to do in situations where the umpires will expect him to co-operate and perhaps to take firm action, for instance

CR-D

in cases of dissent and time-wasting. He will also need to know all about Law 2, which deals with such matters as substitutes.

Law 42 (Unfair Play) states that 'the umpires are the sole judges of fair and unfair play' and that the captains are responsible for seeing that the game is played according to the Laws and in the correct spirit. One of the skipper's most important jobs, therefore, is to make sure that no sharp practice is tolerated, that umpires' decisions are accepted at once and without dissent, that players are not allowed to waste time and that they do not attempt to harass or intimidate the umpire with frivolous or threatening appeals.

The umpires' decision is final, and players must not dispute it. If any player criticises a decision 'by word or action', shows dissent, fails to obey an umpire's instructions or behaves in a way 'which might bring the game into disrepute', the umpire is required to act and the captain is expected to back him up. The umpire will first report the matter to the other umpire, and afterwards to the player's captain. The captain must then do something about it. This should take the form of insisting that the player co-operates at once and apologises to the umpire. If the captain's action has no effect, the umpire must report the incident to 'the Executive of the Player's team and to any Governing Body responsible for the match' for further action. But it is quite clear that the captain should use his authority in support of the umpire to prevent something that may have been said or done only in the heat of the moment from becoming a major incident.

Time-wasting (Law 42.10)

Wasting time is unfair play and is against the spirit of the game. The fielding captain must take responsibility for seeing that his players do not spend too much time polishing the ball as they return it to the bowler, and should make sure that he does not waste time in conferences and in setting the field. The field should not be set in such a way that it takes a long time to cross over between balls, if a left-hander and a right-

hander are batting together, and between overs. If the umpire considers that time-wasting is going on, he will caution the captain of the fielding side and inform the other umpire. If the captain does not get things moving a bit faster, the umpire will give a final caution and report the matter to the batting captain at the next interval. If that does not work, he must report the matter to the authorities, as in other cases of unfair play which umpires and captains together fail to stamp out.

The captain has a clear responsibility here to the spirit of the game rather than to the temporary advantage of his team. He is also responsible for maintaining a decent over rate. If a bowler takes too long to bowl an over and fails to respond to a first and a final warning, the umpire can take action against the bowler, taking him off and not allowing him to bowl again in that innings (Law 42.10 (b)). But the captain should make certain that this is never necessary.

The umpire can also deal with time-wasting by a batsman who may, for instance, have lengthy and frequent conferences with his partner or spend an inordinately long time prodding the pitch. The batsman should be ready to take strike when the bowler is ready to run in. The full procedure for dealing with batsmen who waste time is set out in Law 42.10 and involves cautioning, informing the batting captain at the next interval and reporting finally to competition and team authorities. Again, the captain should never allow his batsmen to waste time, but if they do, he has an early opportunity to put a stop to it.

Substitutes (Law 2)

The fielding side is entitled to a substitute to replace a player who is injured or falls ill in the course of the game — that is, at any time after the teams have been nominated before the start of play. A substitute may field in any position, though the batting captain has the right to object to his keeping wicket. The substitute is not allowed to bat, bowl or act as captain, and if he takes a catch the correct entry in the score book is 'caught sub'.

If, however, a substitute fielder is needed for any reason other than illness or injury, the opposing captain's permission is required. This covers cases where players leave the field to answer the phone, nip down the road to take the washing out of the laundrette or go home to deal with a burst pipe. A player who has been substituted may on recovery or on finding a plumber return to the fray and play a full part in the rest of the match.

Fieldsman leaving the field (Law 2.8)

A fielder who wishes to leave the field must ask the permission of the umpire at the bowler's end, and must ask permission to come back on. If he goes off for more than fifteen minutes, he is not allowed to bowl again on

his return for at least another fifteen. Similarly, if he is off for an hour, he must be on the field for at least another hour before being allowed to bowl again, and so on. If the absence is less than fifteen minutes, however, the returning fielder can bowl again immediately. This Law does not prevent bowlers who arrive late at the start of play from being brought on at once, but it does apply to players returning late after lunch or tea.

Batsman leaving the field or retiring (Law 2.9)

A batsman may leave the field or retire at any time if he is injured or ill or for any 'other unavoidable cause', and has the right to come back at the fall of a wicket or at the retirement of another batsman. If, however, he has left the field for an 'avoidable' reason, he will need the fielding captain's permission to resume his innings.

What is avoidable and what is unavoidable is open to dispute of course. Fred's brother-in-law, Alf, was once called off the field, when he was batting, to answer the phone. The call was from his wife who had locked herself out. As Alf had the keys and the car, he had to go home, still padded up, let her in and drive back. When he turned up at the ground again, a wicket had just fallen but the fielding captain wouldn't let him bat on. He said Alf had left the field for an avoidable reason. Fred, who was captaining us that day, argued that anyone who knew Alf's wife would know that a summons from her was something you avoided at your peril. He managed to blacken his own sister's character so effectively that Alf was allowed to continue his innings and even got a sympathetic round of applause when he walked to the middle. He was out second ball.

The Scorers

One of the many drawbacks of being attached to a cricketer is that if you want to see him during the season, you have to be prepared to sit with frozen fingers for long hours and be a model of accuracy and a mine of information. Occasionally you will be rewarded with a brief nod and a word of thanks. At moments of great triumph someone may even buy you a half of shandy and offer you a crisp.

Tom Smith's *Cricket Umpiring and Scoring* contains much good advice about technique and the Laws affecting scoring, but sufferers from hypothermia and exposure should consult a doctor. This section looks briefly at some of the Laws scorers will need to know about.

The scorers (Law 4)

The Law tells the scorers to check frequently with each other to see that the score sheets agree.

The over (Law 22)

The umpire is responsible for counting the number of balls in the over, and if he miscounts, the scorer must still record the number of balls actually delivered. The umpire is always right. Even scorers married to umpires must accept this for the duration of the match.

Caught (Law 32) and Run out (Law 38)

No runs at all are scored when a batsman is caught, even if the batsmen have completed a run or runs while the ball is in the air. In the case of a run-out, however, all completed runs count. The run being attempted at the time of the run-out does not count, even if the batsmen have crossed. So, if a batsman is run out going for a third run, two runs are scored.

Wide (Law 25) and No ball (Law 24)

The penalty for bowling a wide or a no ball is one run, and this now counts against the bowler. However, if runs are scored by the batsmen running or by the ball reaching the boundary, the penalty run is not added on to them. So, if the batsmen run one for a wide, or a no ball, the total goes up by only one. If the batsmen run two, two are scored (not three).

Batsmen can be run out from wides and no balls and, if that happens, all the completed runs count and are scored as wides or no balls. The penalty run stands if the batsman is run out going for one run off a wide or no ball. If a batsman is out in any other way, for instance stumped off a wide, or hit the ball twice off a no ball, the penalty of one run still stands. If the batsman hits a no ball, any runs are credited to him and not to 'no balls'. In all cases where wide or no ball is called, another ball must be bowled.

Boundaries and overthrows (Law 19)

It is not generally realised that six can be awarded only if the ball has been struck by the batsman. There is no such thing as six wides or six byes. The correct award is only four. However, if the umpire signals six, the dutiful scorer is obliged to record it.

It sometimes happens that when the ball is struck to a distant boundary, the batsmen run five before the ball crosses the line. The batsman then scores five, not four (or nine!). The runs completed above four count, but the four is not added. If only one, two or three have been run at the time the ball goes over the line, the score is four. The run in progress does not count, even if the batsmen have crossed.

The ball may cross the boundary as the result of an overthrow. In this case the runs completed at the instant of the throw count, and so does any run in progress as long as the batsmen have crossed. The four runs for the boundary also count. So if the batsmen have crossed on a second run when the ball is thrown and it goes on to cross the boundary, six runs are scored — one for a completed run, one because the batsmen have crossed at the moment of the throw, and four for the boundary.

Helmets, etc. (Law 41.1)

If the ball strikes a helmet or any other piece of equipment that has been put down somewhere, five runs are added to the runs already scored, including the run in progress if the batsmen have crossed. If the batsman has hit the ball, he is given the five runs and whatever runs have been made before the ball hits the obstruction; if not, they are scored as byes, leg-byes, etc.

Short run (Law 18)

The signal of 'short run' means that only the run being completed is not to be counted. The one the batsman is just starting back for is allowed, although that is actually short too.

In view of the difficulties, demands and discomforts of a scorer's life, humane and enlightened captains may feel that the discretionary shandy-and-crisp allowance should be made a regular thing. Scorers work more willingly if treated with kindness.

FLAHERTY

Close of Play

Here they are, then — edited highlights of the 42 Laws of Cricket. That's thirty-two more than Moses had to deal with. And Moses didn't have to worry about where the bowler's feet landed, whether he was running on to the wicket, where the ball pitched, where it struck the batsman, whether he was playing a stroke, whether the ball would have gone on to hit the stumps, and whether perhaps there was a very faint inside edge on to the pad, all at the same time and with an hysterical bowler at his elbow demanding justice. Moses had only to think about such things as covetousness, murder, adultery and graven images. Child's play.

Some players tend to regard the umpires and the Laws as the natural enemy. But they aren't. Most umpires, despite their physical handicaps and moral failings, are members of the human race. They umpire because, like the players, they love their cricket. And the Laws are there so the game can be played.

Cricket rules — OK?

Cricket Laws

Cricket laws referred to throughout the book are here reproduced, courtesy of MCC.

LAW 2   SUBSTITUTES AND RUNNERS: BATSMAN OR FIELDSMAN LEAVING THE FIELD: BATSMAN RETIRING: BATSMAN COMMENCING INNINGS

1. **Substitutes** Substitutes shall be allowed by right to field for any player who during the match is incapacitated by illness or injury. The consent of the opposing Captain must be obtained for the use of a Substitute if any player is prevented from fielding for any other reason.
2. **Objection to Substitutes** The opposing Captain shall have no right of objection to any player acting as Substitute in the field, nor as to where he shall field, although he may object to the Substitute acting as Wicket-Keeper.
3. **Substitute Not to Bat or Bowl** A Substitute shall not be allowed to bat or bowl.
4. **A Player for whom a Substitute has acted** A player may bat, bowl or field even though a Substitute has acted for him.
5. **Runner** A Runner shall be allowed for a Batsman who during the match is incapacitated by illness or injury. The player acting as Runner shall be a member of the batting side and shall, if possible, have already batted in that innings.
6. **Runner's Equipment** The player acting as Runner for an injured Batsman shall wear batting gloves and pads if the injured Batsman is so equipped.
7. **Transgression of the Laws by an Injured Batsman or Runner** An injured Batsman may be out should his Runner break any one of Laws 33 (Handled the Ball), 37 (Obstructing the Field) or 38 (Run Out). As Striker he remains himself subject to the Laws. Furthermore, should he be out of his ground for any purpose and the wicket at the Wicket-Keeper's end be put down he shall be

out under Law 38 (Run Out) or Law 39 (Stumped) irrespective of the position of the other Batsman or the Runner and no runs shall be scored. When not the Striker, the injured Batsman is out of the game and shall stand where he does not interfere with the play. Should he bring himself into the game in any way then he shall suffer the penalties that any transgression of the Laws demands.

8. Fieldsman Leaving the Field No Fieldsman shall leave the field or return during a session of play without the consent of the Umpire at the Bowler's end. The Umpire's consent is also necessary if a Substitute is required for a Fieldsman, when his side returns to the field after an interval. If a member of the fielding side leaves the field or fails to return after an interval and is absent from the field for longer than 15 minutes, he shall not be permitted to bowl after his return until he has been on the field for at least that length of playing time for which he was absent. This restriction shall not apply at the start of a new day's play.

9. Batsman Leaving the Field or Retiring A Batsman may leave the field or retire at any time owing to illness, injury or other unavoidable cause, having previously notified the Umpire at the Bowler's end. He may resume his innings at the fall of a wicket, which for the purposes of this Law shall include the retirement of another Batsman. If he leaves the field or retires for any other reason he may only resume his innings with the consent of the opposing Captain. When a Batsman has left the field or retired and is unable to return owing to illness, injury or other unavoidable cause, his innings is to be recorded as "retired, not out". Otherwise it is to be recorded as "retired, out".

10. Commencement of a Batsman's Innings A Batsman shall be considered to have commenced his innings once he has stepped on to the field of play.

NOTES (a) Substitutes and Runners *For the purpose of these Laws allowable illnesses or injuries are those which occur at any time after the nomination by the Captains of their teams.*

LAW 3   THE UMPIRES

8. Fitness of Ground, Weather and Light (a) The Umpires shall be the sole judges of the fitness of the ground, weather and light for play. (i) However, before deciding to suspend play or not to start play or not to resume play after an interval or stoppage, the Umpires shall establish whether both Captains (the Batsmen at the wicket may deputise for their Captain) wish to commence or to continue in the prevailing conditions; if so, their wishes shall be met. (ii) In addition, if during play, the Umpires decide that the light is unfit, only the batting side shall have the option of continuing play. After agreeing to continue to play in unfit light conditions, the Captain of the batting side (or a Batsman at the wicket) may appeal against the light to the Umpires, who shall uphold the appeal only if, in their opinion, the light has deteriorated since the agreement to continue was made. (b) After any suspension of play, the Umpires, unaccompanied by any of the Players or Officials shall, on their own initiative, carry out an inspection immediately the conditions improve and shall continue to inspect at intervals. Immediately the Umpires decide that play is possible they shall call upon the Players to resume the game.

LAW 4   THE SCORERS

1. Recording Runs All runs scored shall be recorded by Scorers appointed for the purpose. Where there are two Scorers they shall frequently check to ensure that the score sheets agree.

2. Acknowledging Signals The Scorers shall accept and immediately acknowledge all instructions and signals given to them by the Umpires.

LAW 15   START OF PLAY

1. Call of Play At the start of each innings and of each day's play and on the resumption of play after any interval or interruption the Umpire at the Bowlers' end shall call "play".

2. Practice on the Field At no time on any day of the match shall there be any bowling or batting practice on the pitch. No practice may take place on the field if, in the opinion of the Umpires, it could result in a waste of time.

3. Trial Run-Up No Bowler shall have a trial run-up after "play" has been called in any session of play, except at the fall of a wicket when an Umpire may allow such a trial run-up if he is satisfied that it will not cause any waste of time.

LAW 18   SCORING

1. A Run The score shall be reckoned by runs. A run is scored: (a) So often as the Batsmen, after a hit or at any time while the ball is in play, shall have crossed and made good their ground from end to end. (b) When a boundary is scored. See Law 19 (Boundaries). (c) When penalty runs are awarded. See 6 below.

2. Short Runs (a) If either Batsman runs a short run, the Umpire shall call and signal "one short" as soon as the ball becomes dead and that run shall not be scored. A run is short if a Batsman fails to make good his ground on turning for a further run. (b) Although a short run shortens the succeeding one, the latter, if completed, shall count. (c) If either or both Batsmen deliberately run short the Umpire shall, as soon as he sees that the fielding side have no chance of dismissing either Batsman, call and signal "dead ball" and disallow any runs attempted or previously scored. The Batsmen shall return to their original ends. (d) If both Batsmen run short in one and the same run, only one run shall be deducted. (e) Only if three or more runs are attempted can more than one be short and then, subject to (c) and (d) above, all runs so called shall be disallowed. If there has been more than one short run the Umpires shall instruct the Scorers as to the number of runs disallowed.

3. **Striker Caught** If the Striker is Caught, no run shall be scored.

4. **Batsman Run Out** If a Batsman is Run Out, only that run which was being attempted shall not be scored. If, however, an injured Striker himself is run out no runs shall be scored. See Law 2.7 (Transgression of the Laws by an Injured Batsman or Runner).

5. **Batsman Obstructing the Field** If a Batsman is out Obstructing the Field, any runs completed before the obstruction occurs shall be scored unless such obstruction prevents a catch being made in which case no runs shall be scored.

6. **Runs Scored for Penalties** Runs shall be scored for penalties under Laws 20 (Lost Ball), 24 (No Ball), 25 (Wide Ball), 41.1 (Fielding the Ball) and for boundary allowances under Law 19 (Boundaries).

7. **Batsman Returning to Wicket he has Left** If, while the ball is in play, the Batsmen have crossed in running, neither shall return to the wicket he has left even though a short run has been called or no run has been scored as in the case of a catch. Batsmen, however, shall return to the wickets they originally left in the cases of a boundary and of any disallowance of runs and of an injured Batsman being, himself, run out. See Law 2.7 (Transgression of the Laws by an Injured Batsman or Runner).

NOTES (a) Short Run *A Striker taking stance in front of his popping crease may run from that point without penalty.*

LAW 19   BOUNDARIES

1. **The Boundary of the Playing Area** Before the toss for innings, the Umpires shall agree with both Captains on the boundary of the playing area. The boundary shall, if possible, be marked by a white line, a rope laid on the ground, or a fence. If flags or posts only are used to mark a boundary, the imaginary line joining such points shall be regarded as the boundary. An obstacle, or person, within the playing area shall not be regarded as a boundary unless so decided by the Umpires before the toss for innings. Sight-screens within, or partially within, the playing area shall be regarded as the boundary and when the ball strikes or passes within or under or directly over any part of the screen, a boundary shall be scored.

2. **Runs Scored for Boundaries** Before the toss for innings, the Umpires shall agree with both Captains the runs to be allowed for boundaries, and in deciding the allowance for them, the Umpires and Captains shall be guided by the prevailing custom of the ground. The allowance for a boundary shall normally be 4 runs, and 6 runs for all hits pitching over and clear of the boundary line or fence, even though the ball has been previously touched by a Fieldsman. 6 runs shall also be scored if a Fieldsman, after catching a ball, carries it over the boundary. See Law 32 (Caught), Note (a). 6 runs shall not be scored when a ball struck by the Striker hits a sightscreen full pitch if the screen is within, or partially within, the playing area, but if the ball is struck directly over a sightscreen so situated, 6 runs shall be scored.

3. **A Boundary** A boundary shall be scored and signalled by the Umpire at the Bowler's end whenever, in his opinion: (a) A ball in play touches or crosses the boundary, however marked. (b) A Fieldsman with ball in hand touches or grounds any part of his person on or over a boundary line. (c) A Fieldsman with ball in hand grounds any part of his person over a boundary fence or board. This allows the Fieldsman to touch or lean on or over a boundary fence or board in preventing a boundary.

4. **Runs Exceeding Boundary Allowance** The runs completed at the instant the ball reaches the boundary shall count if they exceed the boundary allowance.

5. **Overthrows or Wilful Act of a Fieldsman** If the boundary results from an overthrow or from the wilful act of a Fieldsman, any runs already completed and the allowance shall be added to the score. The run in progress shall count provided that the Batsmen have crossed at the instant of the throw or act.

NOTES (a) Position of Sight-Screens *Sight-screens should, if possible, be positioned wholly outside the playing area, as near as possible to the boundary line.*

LAW 20   LOST BALL

1. **Runs Scored** If a ball in play cannot be found or recovered any fieldsman may call "lost ball" when 6 runs shall be added to the score; but if more than 6 have been run before "lost ball" is called, as many runs as have been completed shall be scored. The run in progress shall count provided that the Batsmen have crossed at the instant of the call of "lost ball".

2. **How Scored** The runs shall be added to the score of the Striker if the ball has been struck, but otherwise to the score of byes, leg-byes, no-balls or wides as the case may be.

LAW 22   THE OVER

1. **Number of Balls** The ball shall be bowled from each wicket alternately in overs of either 6 or 8 balls according to agreement before the match.
2. **Call of "Over"** When the agreed number of balls has been bowled, and as the ball becomes dead or when it becomes clear to the Umpire at the Bowler's end that both the fielding side and the Batsmen at the wicket have ceased to regard the ball as in play, the Umpire shall call "over" before leaving the wicket.
3. **No Ball or Wide Ball** Neither a no ball nor a wide ball shall be reckoned as one of the over.
4. **Umpire Miscounting** If an Umpire miscounts the number of balls, the over as counted by the Umpire shall stand.
5. **Bowler Changing Ends** A Bowler shall be allowed to change ends as often as desired provided only that he does not bowl two overs consecutively in an innings.
6. **The Bowler Finishing an Over** A Bowler shall finish an over in progress unless he be incapacitated or be suspended under Law 42.8 (The Bowling of Fast Short Pitched Balls), 42.9 (The Bowling of Fast High Full Pitches), 42.10 (Time Wasting) and 42.11 (Players Damaging the Pitch). If an over is left incomplete for any reason at the start of an interval or interruption of play, it shall be finished on the resumption of play.
7. **Bowler Incapacitated or Suspended During an Over** If, for any reason, a Bowler is incapacitated while running up to bowl the first ball of an over, or is incapacitated or suspended during an over, the Umpire shall call and signal "dead ball" and another Bowler shall be allowed to bowl or complete the over from the same end, provided only that he shall not bowl two overs, or part thereof, consecutively in one innings.
8. **Position of Non-Striker** The Batsman at the Bowler's end shall normally stand on the opposite side of the wicket to that from which the ball is being delivered, unless a request to do otherwise is granted by the Umpire.

LAW 23   DEAD BALL

1. **The Ball Becomes Dead, when:** (a) It is finally settled in the hands of the Wicket-Keeper or the Bowler. (b) It reaches or pitches over the boundary. (c) A Batsman is out. (d) Whether played or not, it lodges in the clothing or equipment of a Batsman or the clothing of an Umpire. (e) A ball lodges in a protective helmet worn by a member of the fielding side. (f) A penalty is awarded under Law 20 (Lost Ball) or Law 41.1 (Fielding the Ball). (g) The Umpire calls "over" or "time".
2. **Either Umpire Shall Call and Signal "Dead Ball", when:** (a) He intervenes in a case of unfair play. (b) A serious injury to a Player or Umpire occurs. (c) He is satisfied that, for an adequate reason, the Striker is not ready to receive the ball and makes no attempt to play it. (d) The Bowler drops the ball accidentally before delivery, or the ball does not leave his hand for any reason. (e) One or both bails fall from the Striker's wicket before he receives delivery. (f) He leaves his normal position for consultation. (g) He is required to do so under Law 26.3 (Disallowance of Leg-Byes), etc.
3. **The Ball Ceases to be Dead, when:** (a) The Bowler starts his run up or bowling action.
4. **The Ball is Not Dead, when:** (a) It strikes an Umpire (unless it lodges in his dress). (b) The wicket is broken or struck down (unless a Batsman is out thereby). (c) An unsuccessful appeal is made. (d) The wicket is broken accidentally either by the Bowler during his delivery or by a Batsman in running. (d) The Umpire has called "no ball" or "wide".
NOTES (a) Ball finally Settled *Whether the ball is finally settled or not (see 1 (a) above) must be a question for the Umpires alone to decide.* (b) Action on Call of "Dead Ball" *(i) If "dead ball" is called prior to the Striker receiving a delivery the Bowler shall be allowed an additional ball. (ii) If "dead ball" is called after the Striker receives a delivery the Bowler shall not be allowed an additional ball, unless a "no ball" or "wide" has been called.*

LAW 24   NO BALL

1. **Mode of Delivery** The Umpire shall indicate to the Striker whether the Bowler intends to bowl over or round the wicket, overarm or underarm, or right- or left-handed. Failure on the part of the Bowler to indicate in advance a change in his mode of delivery is unfair and the Umpire shall call and signal "no ball".
2. **Fair Delivery — The Arm** For a delivery to be fair the ball must be bowled not thrown — see Note (a) below. If either Umpire is not entirely satisfied with the absolute fairness of a delivery in this respect he shall call and signal "no ball" instantly upon delivery.
3. **Fair Delivery — The Feet** The Umpire at the bowler's wicket shall call and signal "no ball" if he is not satisfied that in the delivery stride: (a) the Bowler's back foot has landed within and not touching the return crease or its forward extension, *or* (b) some part of the front foot whether grounded or raised was behind the popping crease.

4. Bowler Throwing at Striker's Wicket Before Delivery If the Bowler, before delivering the ball, throws it at the Striker's wicket in an attempt to run him out, the Umpire shall call and signal "no ball". See Law 42.12 (Batsman Unfairly Stealing a Run) and Law 38 (Run Out).

5. Bowler Attempting to Run Out Non-Striker Before Delivery If the Bowler, before delivering the ball, attempts to run out the non-Striker, any runs which result shall be allowed and shall be scored as no balls. Such an attempt shall not count as a ball in the over. The Umpire shall not call "no ball". See Law 42.12 (Batsman Unfairly Stealing a Run).

6. Infringement of Laws by a Wicket-Keeper or a Fieldsman The Umpire shall call and signal "no ball" in the event of the Wicket-Keeper infringing Law 40.1 (Position of Wicket Keeper) or a Fieldsman infringing Law 41.2 (Limitation of On-side Fieldsmen) or Law 41.3 (Position of Fieldsmen).

7. Revoking a Call An Umpire shall revoke the call "no ball" if the ball does not leave the Bowler's hand for any reason. See Law 23.2 (Either Umpire Shall Call and Signal "Dead Ball").

8. Penalty A penalty of one run for a no ball shall be scored if no runs are made otherwise.

9. Runs From a No Ball The Striker may hit a no ball and whatever runs result shall be added to his score. Runs made otherwise from a no ball shall be scored no balls.

10. Out From a No Ball The Striker shall be out from a no ball if he breaks Law 34 (Hit the Ball Twice) and either Batsman may be Run Out or shall be given out if either breaks Law 33 (Handled the Ball) or Law 37 (Obstructing the Field).

11. Batsman Given Out Off a No Ball Should a Batsman be given out off a no ball the penalty for bowling it shall stand unless runs are otherwise scored.

NOTES (a) Definition of a Throw *A ball shall be deemed to have been thrown if, in the opinion of either Umpire, the process of straightening the bowling arm, whether it be partial or complete, takes place during that part of the delivery swing which directly precedes the ball leaving the hand. This definition shall not debar a Bowler from the use of the wrist in the delivery swing.* (b) No Ball not Counting in Over *A no ball shall not be reckoned as one of the over. See Law 22.3 (No Ball or Wide Ball).*

LAW 25   WIDE BALL

1. Judging a Wide If the Bowler bowls the ball so high over or so wide of the wicket that, in the opinion of the Umpire it passes out of reach of the Striker, standing in a normal guard position, the Umpire shall call and signal "wide ball" as soon as it has passed the line of the Striker's wicket. The Umpire shall not adjudge a ball as being a wide if: (a) The Striker, by moving from his guard position, causes the ball to pass out of his reach. (b) The Striker moves and thus brings the ball within his reach.

2. Penalty A penalty of one run for a wide shall be scored if no runs are made otherwise.

3. Ball Coming to Rest in Front of the Striker If a ball which the Umpire considers to have been delivered comes to rest in front of the line of the Striker's wicket, "wide" shall not be called. The Striker has a right, without interference from the fielding side, to make one attempt to hit the ball. If the fielding side interfere, the Umpire shall replace the ball where it came to rest and shall order the Fieldsmen to resume the places they occupied in the field before the ball was delivered. The Umpire shall call and signal "dead ball" as soon as it is clear that the Striker does not intend to hit the ball, or after the Striker has made one unsuccessful attempt to hit the ball.

4. Revoking a Call The Umpire shall revoke the call if the Striker hits a ball which has been called "wide".

5. Ball Not Dead The ball does not become dead on the call of "wide ball" — see Law 23.4 (The Ball is Not Dead).

6. Runs Resulting from a Wide All runs which are run or result from a wide ball which is not a no ball shall be scored wide balls, or if no runs are made one shall be scored.

7. Out from a Wide The Striker shall be out from a wide ball if he breaks Law 35 (Hit Wicket) or Law 39 (Stumped). Either Batsman may be Run Out and shall be out if he breaks Law 33 (Handled the Ball) or Law 37 (Obstructing the Field).

8. Batsman Given Out Off a Wide Should a Batsman be given out off a wide, the penalty for bowling it shall stand unless runs are otherwise made.

NOTES (a) Wide Ball not Counting in Over *A wide ball shall not be reckoned as one of the over — see Law 22.3 (No Ball or Wide Ball).*

LAW 26   BYE AND LEG-BYE

1. Byes If the ball, not having been called "wide" or "no ball", passes the Striker without touching his bat or person, and any runs are obtained, the Umpire shall signal "bye" and the run or runs shall be credited as such to the batting side.

2. Leg-Byes If the ball, not having been called "wide" or "no ball" is unintentionally deflected by the Striker's dress or person, except a hand holding the bat, and any runs are obtained the Umpire shall signal "leg-bye" and the run or runs so scored shall be credited as such to the batting side. Such leg-byes shall only be scored if, in the opinion of the Umpire, the Striker has: (a) attempted to play the ball with his bat, *or* (b) tried to avoid being hit by the ball.

3. Disallowance of Leg-Byes In the case of a deflection by the Striker's person, other than in 2(a) and (b) above, the Umpire shall call and signal "dead ball" as soon as one run has been completed or when it is clear that a run is not being attempted or the ball has reached the boundary. On the call and signal of "dead ball" the Batsmen shall return to their original ends and no runs shall be allowed.

LAW 27   APPEALS

1. Time of Appeals The Umpires shall not give a Batsman out unless appealed to by the other side which shall be done prior to the Bowler beginning his run-up or bowling action to deliver the next ball. Under Law 23.1(g) (The Ball Becomes Dead) the ball is dead on "over" being called; this does not, however, invalidate an appeal made prior to the first ball of the following over provided "time" has not been called.

2. An Appeal "How's That?" An appeal "How's That?" shall cover all ways of being out.

3. Answering Appeals The Umpire at the Bowler's wicket shall answer appeals before the other Umpire in all cases except those arising out of Law 35 (Hit Wicket) or Law 39 (Stumped) or Law 38 (Run Out) when this occurs at the Striker's wicket. When either Umpire has given a Batsman not out, the other Umpire shall, within his jurisdiction, answer the appeal or a further appeal, provided it is made in time in accordance with 1 above (Time of Appeals).

4. Consultation by Umpires An Umpire may consult with the other Umpire on a point of fact which the latter may have been in a better position to see and shall then give his decision. If, after consultation, there is still doubt remaining the decision shall be in favour of the Batsman.

5. Batsman Leaving his Wicket under a Misapprehension The Umpires shall intervene if satisfied that a Batsman, not having been given out, has left his wicket under a misapprehension that he has been dismissed.

6. Umpire's Decision The Umpire's decision is final. He may alter his decision, provided that such alteration is made promptly.

7. Withdrawal of an Appeal In exceptional circumstances the Captain of the fielding side may seek permission of the Umpire to withdraw an appeal providing the outgoing Batsman has not left the playing area. If this is allowed, the Umpire shall cancel his decision.

LAW 28   THE WICKET IS DOWN

1. Wicket Down The wicket is down if: (a) Either the ball or the Striker's bat or person completely removes either bail from the top of the stumps. A disturbance of a bail, whether temporary or not, shall not constitute a complete removal, but the wicket is down if a bail in falling lodges between two of the stumps. (b) Any player completely removes with his hand or arm a bail from the top of the stumps, providing that the ball is held in that hand or in the hand of the arm so used. (c) When both bails are off, a stump is struck out of the ground by the ball, or a player strikes or pulls a stump out of the ground, providing that the ball is held in the hand(s) or in the hand of the arm so used.

2. One Bail Off If one bail is off, it shall be sufficient for the purpose of putting the wicket down to remove the remaining bail, or to strike or pull any of the three stumps out of the ground in any of the ways stated in 1 above.

3. All the Stumps Out of the Ground If all the stumps are out of the ground, the fielding side shall be allowed to put back one or more stumps in order to have an opportunity of putting the wicket down.

4. Dispensing with Bails If owing to the strength of the wind, it has been agreed to dispense with the bails in accordance with Law 8 Note (a) (Dispensing with Bails), the decision as to when the wicket is down is one for the Umpires to decide on the facts before them. In such circumstances and if the Umpires so decide the wicket shall be held to be down even though a stump has not been struck out of the ground.

NOTES (a) Remaking the Wicket *If the wicket is broken while the ball is in play, it is not the Umpire's duty to remake the wicket until the ball has become dead — see Law 23 (Dead Ball). A member of the fielding side, however, may remake the wicket in such circumstances.*

LAW 29   BATSMAN OUT OF HIS GROUND

1. When out of his Ground A Batsman shall be considered to be out of his ground unless some part of his bat in his hand or of his person is grounded behind the line of the popping crease.

LAW 30   BOWLED

1. Out Bowled The Striker shall be out bowled if: (a) His wicket is bowled down, even if the ball first touches his bat or person. (b) He breaks his wicket by hitting or kicking the ball on to it before the completion of a stroke, or as a result of attempting to guard his wicket. See Law 34.1 (Out — Hit the Ball Twice).

NOTES (a) Out Bowled — Not LBW *The Striker is out Bowled if the ball is deflected on to his wicket even though a decision against him would be justified under Law 36 (Leg Before Wicket).*

LAW 31   TIMED OUT

1. **Out Timed Out** An incoming Batsman shall be out Timed Out if he wilfully takes more than two minutes to come in — the two minutes being timed from the moment a wicket falls until the new batsman steps on to the field of play. If this is not complied with and if the Umpire is satisfied that the delay was wilful and if an appeal is made, the new Batsman shall be given out by the Umpire at the Bowler's end.
2. **Time to be Added** The time taken by the Umpires to investigate the cause of the delay shall be added at the normal close of play.

NOTES (a) Entry in Score Book *The correct entry in the score book when a Batsman is given out under this Law is "timed out", and the Bowler does not get credit for the wicket.* (b) Batsmen Crossing on the Field of Play *It is an essential duty of the Captains to ensure that the in-going Batsman passes the out-going one before the latter leaves the field of play.*

LAW 32   CAUGHT

1. **Out Caught** The Striker shall be out Caught if the ball touches his bat or if it touches below the wrist his hand or glove, holding the bat, and is subsequently held by a Fieldsman before it touches the ground.
2. **A Fair Catch** A catch shall be considered to have been fairly made if: (a) The Fieldsman is within the field of play throughout the act of making the catch. (i) The act of making the catch shall start from the time when the Fieldsman first handles the ball and shall end when he both retains complete control over the further disposal of the ball and remains within the field of play. (ii) In order to be within the field of play, the Fieldsman may not touch or ground any part of his person on or over a boundary line. When the boundary is marked by a fence or board the Fieldsman may not ground any part of his person over the boundary fence or board, but may touch or lean over the boundary fence or board in completing the catch. (b) The ball is hugged to the body of the catcher or accidentally lodges in his dress or, in the case of the Wicket-Keeper, in his pads. However, a Striker may not be caught if a ball lodges in a protective helmet worn by a Fieldsman, in which case the Umpire shall call and signal "dead ball". See Law 23 (Dead Ball) (c) The ball does not touch the ground even though a hand holding it does so in effecting the catch. (d) A Fieldsman catches the ball, after it has been lawfully played a second time by the Striker, but only if the ball has not touched the ground since being first struck. (e) A Fieldsman catches the ball after it has touched an Umpire, another Fieldsman or the other Batsman. However, a Striker may not be caught if a ball has touched a protective helmet worn by a Fieldsman. (f) The ball is caught off an obstruction within the boundary provided it has not previously been agreed to regard the obstruction as a boundary.
3. **Scoring of Runs** If a Striker is caught, no runs shall be scored.

NOTES (a) Scoring from an Attempted Catch *When a Fieldsman carrying the ball touches or grounds any part of his person on or over a boundary marked by a line, 6 runs shall be scored.* (b) Ball Still in Play *If a Fieldsman releases the ball before he crosses the boundary, the ball will be considered to be still in play and it may be caught by another Fieldsman. However, if the original Fieldsman returns to the field of play and handles the ball, a catch may not be made.*

LAW 33   HANDLED THE BALL

1. **Out Handled the Ball** Either Batsman on appeal shall be out Handled the Ball if he wilfully touches the ball while in play with the hand not holding the bat unless he does so with the consent of the opposite side.

NOTES (a) Entry in Score Book *The correct entry in the score book when a Batsman is given out under this Law is "handled the ball", and the Bowler does not get credit for the wicket.*

LAW 34   HIT THE BALL TWICE

1. **Out Hit the Ball Twice** The Striker, on appeal, shall be out Hit the Ball Twice if, after the ball is struck or is stopped by any part of his person, he wilfully strikes it again with his bat or person except for the sole purpose of guarding his wicket: this he may do with his bat or any part of his person other than his hands, but see Law 37.2 (Obstructing a Ball From Being Caught). For the purpose of this Law, a hand holding the bat shall be regarded as part of the bat.
2. **Returning the Ball to a Fieldsman** The Striker, on appeal, shall be out under this Law, if, without the consent of the opposite side, he uses his bat or person to return the ball to any of the fielding side.
3. **Runs from Ball Lawfully Struck Twice** No runs except those which result from an overthrow or penalty, see Law 41 (The Fieldsman), shall be scored from a ball lawfully struck twice.

NOTES (a) Entry in Score Book *The correct entry in the score book when the Striker is given out under this Law is "hit the ball twice", and the Bowler does not get credit for the wicket.* (b) Runs Credited to the Batsman *Any runs awarded under 3 above as a result of an overthrow or penalty shall be credited to the Striker, provided the ball in the first instance has touched the bat, or, if otherwise as extras.*

LAW 35   HIT WICKET

1. **Out Hit Wicket** The Striker shall be out Hit Wicket if, while the ball is in play: (a) His wicket is broken with any part of his person, dress, or equipment as a result of any action taken by him in preparing to receive or in receiving a delivery, or in setting off for his first run, immediately after playing, or playing at, the ball. (b) He hits down his wicket whilst lawfully making a second stroke for the purpose of guarding his wicket within the provisions of Law 34.1 (Out Hit the Ball Twice).

NOTES (a) Not Out Hit Wicket *A Batsman is not out under this Law should his wicket be broken in any of the ways referred to in 1(a) above if: (i) It occurs while he is in the act of running, other than in setting off for his first run immediately after playing at the ball, or while he is avoiding being run out or stumped. (ii) The Bowler after starting his run-up or bowling action does not deliver the ball; in which case the Umpire shall immediately call and signal "dead ball". (iii) It occurs whilst he is avoiding a throw-in at any time.*

LAW 36   LEG BEFORE WICKET

1. **Out LBW** The Striker shall be out LBW in the circumstances set out below: (a) **Striker Attempting to Play the Ball** The Striker shall be out LBW if he first intercepts with any part of his person, dress or equipment a fair ball which would have hit the wicket and which has not previously touched his bat or a hand holding the bat, provided that: (i) The ball pitched, in a straight line between wicket and wicket or on the off side of the Striker's wicket, or in the case of a ball intercepted full pitch would have pitched in a straight line between wicket and wicket; and (ii) the point of impact is in a straight line between wicket and wicket, even if above the level of the bails. (b) **Striker Making No Attempt to Play the Ball** The Striker shall be out LBW even if the ball is intercepted outside the line of the off-stump, if, in the opinion of the Umpire, he has made no genuine attempt to play the ball with his bat, but has intercepted the ball with some part of his person and if the circumstances set out in (a) above apply.

LAW 37   OBSTRUCTING THE FIELD

1. **Wilful Obstruction** Either Batsman, on appeal, shall be out Obstructing the Field if he wilfully obstructs the opposite side by word or action.
2. **Obstructing a Ball from Being Caught** The Striker, on appeal, shall be out should wilful obstruction by either Batsman prevent a catch being made. This shall apply even though the Striker causes the obstruction in lawfully guarding his wicket under the provisions of Law 34. See Law 34.1 (Out Hit the Ball Twice).

NOTES (a) Accidental Obstruction *The Umpires must decide whether the obstruction was wilful or not. The accidental interception of a throw-in by a Batsman while running does not break this Law.* (b) Entry in Score Book *The correct entry in the score book when a Batsman is given out under this Law is "obstructing the field", and the bowler does not get credit for the wicket.*

LAW 38   RUN OUT

1. **Out Run Out** Either Batsman shall be out Run Out if in running or at any time while the ball is in play — except in the circumstances described in Law 39 (Stumped) — he is out of his ground and his wicket is put down by the opposite side. If, however, a Batsman in running makes good his ground he shall not be out Run Out, if he subsequently leaves his ground, to avoid injury, and the wicket is put down.
2. **"No Ball" Called** If a no ball has been called, the Striker shall not be given Run Out unless he attempts to run.
3. **Which Batsman is Out** If the Batsmen have crossed in running, he who runs for the wicket which is put down shall be out; if they have not crossed, he who has left the wicket which is put down shall be out. If a Batsman remains in his ground or returns to his ground and the other Batsman joins him there, the latter shall be out if his wicket is put down.
4. **Scoring of Runs** If a Batsman is run out, only that run which is being attempted shall not be scored. If however an injured Striker himself is run out, no runs shall be scored. See Law 2.7 (Transgression of the Laws by an Injured Batsman or Runner).

NOTES (a) Ball Played on to Opposite Wicket *If the ball is played on to the opposite wicket neither Batsman is liable to be Run Out unless the ball has been touched by a Fieldsman before the wicket is broken.* (b) Entry in Score Book *The correct entry in the score book when the Striker is given out under this Law is "run out", and the Bowler does not get credit for the wicket.*

LAW 39   STUMPED

1. **Out Stumped** The Striker shall be out Stumped if, in receiving a ball, not being a no ball, he is out of his ground otherwise than in attempting a run and the wicket is put down by the Wicket-Keeper without the intervention of another Fieldsman.
2. **Action by the Wicket-Keeper** The Wicket-Keeper may take the ball in front of the wicket in an attempt to Stump the Striker only if the ball has touched the bat or person of the Striker.

NOTES (a) Ball Rebounding from Wicket-Keeper's Person *The Striker may be out Stumped if in the circumstances stated in 1 above, the wicket is broken by a ball rebounding from the Wicket-Keeper's person or equipment or is kicked or thrown by the Wicket-Keeper on to the wicket.*

LAW 40   THE WICKET-KEEPER

1. **Position of Wicket-Keeper** The Wicket-Keeper shall remain wholly behind the wicket until a ball delivered by the Bowler touches the bat or person of the Striker, or passes the wicket, or until the Striker attempts a run. In the event of the Wicket-Keeper contravening this Law, the Umpire at the Striker's end shall call and signal "no ball" at the instant of delivery or as soon as possible thereafter.
2. **Restriction on Actions of the Wicket-Keeper** If the Wicket-Keeper interferes with the striker's right to play the ball and to guard his wicket, the Striker shall not be out, except under Laws 33 (Handled the Ball), 34 (Hit the Ball Twice), 37 (Obstructing the Field) and 38 (Run Out).
3. **Interference with the Wicket-Keeper by the Striker** If in the legitimate defence of his wicket, the Striker interferes with the Wicket-Keeper, he shall not be out, except as provided for in Law 37.2 (Obstructing a Ball From Being Caught).

LAW 41   THE FIELDSMAN

1. **Fielding the Ball** The Fieldsman may stop the ball with any part of his person, but if he wilfully stops it otherwise, 5 runs shall be added to the run or runs already scored; if no run has been scored 5 penalty runs shall be awarded. The run in progress shall count provided that the Batsmen have crossed at the instant of the act. If the ball has been struck, the penalty shall be added to the score of the Striker, but otherwise to the score of byes, leg-byes, no balls or wides as the case may be.
2. **Limitation of On-Side Fieldsmen** The number of on-side Fieldsmen behind the popping crease at the instant of the Bowler's delivery shall not exceed two. In the event of infringement by the fielding side the Umpire at the Striker's end shall call and signal "no ball" at the instant of delivery or as soon as possible thereafter.
3. **Position of Fieldsmen** Whilst the ball is in play and until the ball has made contact with the bat or the Striker's person or has passed his bat, no Fieldsman, other than the Bowler, may stand on or have any part of his person extended over the pitch (measuring 22 yards/20.12m x 10ft/3.05m). In the event of a Fieldsman contravening this Law, the Umpire at the bowler's end shall call and signal "no ball" at the instant of delivery or as soon as possible thereafter. See Law 40.1 (Position of Wicket-Keeper).

NOTES (a) Batsmen Changing Ends *The 5 runs referred to in 1 above are a penalty and the batsmen do not change ends solely by reason of this penalty.*

LAW 42   UNFAIR PLAY

1. **Responsibility of Captains** The Captains are responsible at all times for ensuring that play is conducted within the spirit of the game as well as within the Laws.
2. **Responsibility of Umpires** The Umpires are the sole judges of fair and unfair play.
3. **Intervention by the Umpire** The Umpires shall intervene without appeal by calling and signalling "dead ball" in the case of unfair play, but should not otherwise interfere with the progress of the game except as required to do so by the Laws.
4. **Lifting the Seam** A Player shall not lift the seam of the ball for any reason. Should this be done, the Umpires shall change the ball for one of similar condition to that in use prior to the contravention. See Note (a).
5. **Changing the Condition of the Ball** Any member of the fielding side may polish the ball provided that such polishing wastes no time and that no artificial substance is used. No one shall rub the ball on the ground or use any artificial substance or take any other action to alter the condition of the ball. In the event of a contravention of this Law, the Umpires, after consultation, shall change the ball for one of similar condition to that in use prior to the contravention. This Law does not prevent a member of the fielding side from drying a wet ball, or removing mud from the ball. See Note (b).

6. Incommoding the Striker An Umpire is justified in intervening under this Law and shall call and signal "dead ball" if, in his opinion, any Player of the fielding side incommodes the Striker by any noise or action while he is receiving a ball.

7. Obstruction of a Batsman in Running It shall be considered unfair if any Fieldsman wilfully obstructs a Batsman in running. In these circumstances the Umpire shall call and signal "dead ball" and allow any completed runs and the run in progress or alternatively any boundary scored.

8. The Bowling of Fast Short Pitched Balls The bowling of fast short pitched balls is unfair if, in the opinion of the Umpire at the Bowler's end, it constitutes an attempt to intimidate the Striker. See Note (d). Umpires shall consider intimidation to be the deliberate bowling of fast short pitched balls which by their length, height and direction are intended or likely to inflict physical injury on the Striker. The relative skill of the Striker shall also be taken into consideration. In the event of such unfair bowling, the Umpire at the Bowler's end shall adopt the following procedure: (a) In the first instance the Umpire shall call and signal "no ball", caution the Bowler and inform the other Umpire, the Captain of the fielding side and the Batsmen of what has occurred. (b) If this caution is ineffective, he shall repeat the above procedure and indicate to the Bowler that this is a final warning. (c) Both the above caution and final warning shall continue to apply even though the Bowler may later change ends. (d) Should the above warnings prove ineffective the Umpire at the Bowler's end shall: (i) At the first repetition call and signal "no ball" and when the ball is dead direct the Captain to take the Bowler off forthwith and to complete the over with another Bowler, provided that the Bowler does not bowl two overs or part thereof consecutively. See Law 22.7 (Bowler Incapacitated or Suspended during an Over). (ii) Not allow the Bowler, thus taken off, to bowl again in the same innings. (iii) Report the occurrence to the Captain of the batting side as soon as the Players leave the field for an interval. (iv) Report the occurrence to the Executive of the fielding side and to any governing body responsible for the match who shall take any further action which is considered to be appropriate against the Bowler concerned.

9. The Bowling of Fast High Full Pitches The bowling of fast high full pitches is unfair. See Note (e). In the event of such unfair bowling the Umpire at the bowler's end shall adopt the procedures of caution, final warning, action against the Bowler and reporting as set out in 8 above.

10. Time Wasting Any form of time wasting is unfair. (a) In the event of the Captain of the fielding side wasting time or allowing any member of his side to waste time, the Umpire at the Bowler's end shall adopt the following procedure: (i) In the first instance he shall caution the Captain of the fielding side and inform the other Umpire of what has occurred. (ii) If this caution is ineffective he shall repeat the above procedure and indicate to the Captain that this is a final warning. (iii) The Umpire shall report the occurrence to the Captain of the batting side as soon as the Players leave the field for an interval. (iv) Should the above procedure prove ineffective the Umpire shall report the occurrence to the Executive of the fielding side and to any governing body responsible for that match who shall take appropriate action against the Captain and the Players concerned. (b) In the event of a Bowler taking unnecessarily long to bowl an over the Umpire at the Bowler's end shall adopt the procedures, other than the calling of "no ball", of caution, final warning, action against the Bowler and reporting. (c) In the event of a Batsman wasting time (see Note (f)) other than in the manner described in Law 31 (Timed Out), the Umpire at the Bowler's end shall adopt the following procedure: (i) In the first instance he shall caution the batsman and inform the other Umpire at once, and the Captain of the batting side, as soon as the Players leave the field for an interval, of what has occurred. (ii) If this proves ineffective, he shall repeat the caution, indicate to the Batsman that this is a final warning and inform the other Umpire. (iii) The Umpire shall report the occurrence to both Captains as soon as the Players leave the field for an interval. (iv) Should the above procedure prove ineffective, the Umpire shall report the occurrence to the Executive of the batting side and to any governing body responsible for that match who shall take appropriate action against the Player concerned.

11. Players Damaging the Pitch The Umpires shall intervene and prevent Players from causing damage to the pitch which may assist the Bowlers of either side. See Note (c). (a) In the event of any member of the fielding side damaging the pitch the Umpire shall follow the procedure of caution, final warning and reporting as set out in 10(a) above. (b) In the event of a Bowler contravening this Law by running down the pitch after delivering the ball, the Umpire at the Bowler's end shall first caution the Bowler. If this caution is ineffective the Umpire shall adopt the procedures, other than the calling of "no ball", of final warning, action against the Bowler and reporting. (c) In the event of a Batsman damaging the pitch the Umpire at the Bowler's end shall follow the procedures of caution, final warning and reporting as set out in 10(c) above.

12. Batsman Unfairly Stealing a Run Any attempt by the Batsman to steal a run during the Bowler's run-up is unfair. Unless the Bowler attempts to run out either Batsman — see Law 24.4 (Bowler Throwing at Striker's Wicket Before Delivery) and Law 24.5 (Bowler Attempting to Run Out Non-Striker Before Delivery) — the Umpire shall call and signal "dead ball" as soon as the Batsmen cross in any such attempt to run. The Batsmen shall then return to their original wickets.

13. Players' Conduct In the event of a player failing to comply with the instructions of an Umpire, criticising his decisions by word or action, or showing dissent, or generally behaving in a manner which might bring the game into disrepute, the Umpire concerned shall, in the first place report the matter to the other Umpire and to the Player's Captain requesting the latter to take action.

If this proves ineffective, the Umpire shall report the incident as soon as possible to the Executive of the Player's team and to any Governing Body responsible for the match, who shall take any further action which is considered appropriate against the Player or Players concerned.

NOTES (a) The Condition of the Ball *Umpires shall make frequent and irregular inspections of the condition of the ball.* (b) Drying of a Wet Ball *A wet ball may be dried on a towel or with sawdust.* (c) Danger Area *The danger area on the pitch, which must be protected from damage by a Bowler, shall be regarded by the Umpires as the area contained by an imaginary line 4ft/1.22m from the popping crease, and parallel to it, and within two imaginary and parallel lines drawn down the pitch from points on that line 1ft/30.48cm on either side of the middle stump.* (d) Fast Short Pitched Balls *As a guide, a fast short pitched ball is one which pitches short and passes, or would have passed, above the shoulder height of the Striker standing in a normal batting stance at the crease.* (e) The Bowling of Fast Full Pitches *The bowling of one fast, high full pitch shall be considered to be unfair if, in the opinion of the Umpire, it is deliberate, bowled at the Striker, and if it passes or would have passed above the shoulder height of the Striker when standing in a normal batting stance at the crease.* (f) Time Wasting by Batsmen *Other than in exceptional circumstances, the Batsman should always be ready to take strike when the Bowler is ready to start his run-up.*

Index